IT'S
MY TURN
NOW

Odell Cleveland

It's My Turn Now by Odell Cleveland.

©2020 Odell Cleveland

Odell@odellcleveland.com
www.OdellCleveland.com

ISBN: 978-1-7340033-0-7

"To everything there is a season,

A time for every purpose under heaven."

To Glen and Noddy:

During this season of shared caregiving, it is a blessing when
siblings are able to work together to care for the mother who
birthed, nurtured, cared for and loved them unconditionally.
Though no longer with us, we know that Nay also would have done
all she could to help during this season of caregiving.

CONTENTS

IT'S
MY TURN
NOW

PREFACE

As a child, I loved when it was my turn.

It's my turn now. The very thought of it excited me. My mother, Glenda Adams Cleveland, spent many hours teaching my three siblings and me about sharing, including how to stand patiently in line while others took their turns. She assured us that our waiting would be rewarded when we reached the front of the line and heard the magic words: "Who's next?" A wide grin would spread across my face, revealing my dimples, as I would raise my hand and shout, "Me! Me! I'm next!" And as she stood holding my hand in line, she would say softly and sweetly, "It's Dell's turn now."

Mommy always tried to make sure life gave her four children a fair turn even as she struggled with her own adversities. A divorced single mother in our hometown of Charleston, S.C., she suffered a massive stroke at age 25 that left her physically disabled. Though it made her life difficult, it never affected the care and devotion she showed her children. When I was in the third grade, she walked three miles — a wooden cane in her right hand and a long metal brace strapped to her left leg — to make sure I wasn't shunted off to a special education class. When I was a star player on Middleton High School's 1977 state championship basketball team, Mommy somehow managed to find her way to the gym for every game, lending her voice and energy from a seat in the bleachers.

Her journey from tragedy to triumph, an inspiring testament to the power of faith and hard work, taught me that the pathway to prosperity is a hand up, not a handout. We might have been born into poverty and public housing, she told us, but we could achieve anything we desired if we would do three things: Trust in God. Get the best education available to us. Never look down on others.

Mommy was right, as she so often is. Faith, education and compassion were the common denominators in all of my life's successes — from co-founding a nationally recognized nonprofit to helping lead one of the largest churches in Greensboro, N.C. My accomplishments are a testimony to my mother's influence and wisdom. I share them not to brag, but to demonstrate the profound impact her words and actions had on me.

In 1984, I graduated with a bachelor's degree in management from the University of South Carolina Spartanburg (now USC Upstate). I was captain of the 1983 NAIA national championship basketball team and was inducted into the USC Upstate Athletics Hall of Fame. An ordained Baptist minister, I received a master of divinity degree with honors from Hood Theological Seminary in 1997 and attended Harvard Divinity School's Summer Leadership Institute. The Charleston Chapter of the National Epicureans Inc. honored me with its Pinnacle Award for Community Impact, and Triad Business Journal named me one of Central North Carolina's most influential people.

Given my upbringing, I am perhaps most proud of the 16 years I spent as chief executive officer of the Welfare Reform Liaison Project, a faith-based nonprofit I co-founded in 1997. The project, born out of my master's thesis on tackling barriers to self-sufficiency, provided job training and other essential skills to people on welfare entering the workforce. We were honored to receive national attention: The U.S. Department of Housing and Urban Development named WRLP one of the nation's 200 best organizations for community building. In 2011, Oxford University Press published a history of WRLP that I co-authored: "Pracademics and Community Change: A True Story of Nonprofit Development and Social Entrepreneurship During Welfare Reform." In 2016, U.S. Rep. Mark Walker, then a Republican congressman representing Greensboro, invited me to be a guest at the State of the Union address.

Today, I'm chief administrative officer of Mount Zion Baptist Church of Greensboro, a 6,000-member predominantly African-American church founded in 1900. And I remain committed to finding common ground around important issues. My perspective on health care and poverty has led a diverse array of national leaders to seek my viewpoint – from former House Speaker Paul Ryan to Melissa Rogers, director of the Office of Faith-based and Neighborhood Partnerships during the Obama administration.

Yes, I stay busy, but Mommy is never far from my mind. The years have taken a toll on her health, requiring me to return to Charleston more frequently to care for her while juggling a demanding yet rewarding career. During a recent flight home from an interfaith study mission in Israel, I asked myself this question: "If one poor, divorced, single mother who suffered a massive stroke could take care of four children, why can't the three surviving children take care of one mother?"

It's my turn now. That's the feeling I frequently experience as Mommy's caregiver. But it's not the same sensation I had as a kid — loving the very thought of being next in line. The excitement, joy and rewards aren't the same.

My younger brother Vernard — we call him "Noddy" — is a civil engineer who sacrificed many professional and personal opportunities to live with Mommy as her primary caregiver. Each weekday morning, Mommy gets ready at 6 a.m. for the van that takes her to a senior day care facility while Noddy goes to work. My older sister Glenda, also known as "Glen," lives 20 minutes away. Together, they do a tremendous job of taking care of Mommy's day-to-day needs, which allows her to remain in her home with Noddy.

As the years have progressed, Glen has developed health challenges of her own and Noddy will be retiring soon and moving on with his life.

As the long-distance member of Mommy's caregiving team — and the sibling who has power of attorney — I called a family team meeting for all four of us to discuss Noddy's retirement plans. I explained the situation to Mommy and Glen, then thanked Noddy for the tremendous job he has done caring for Mommy. After I finished, Glen also thanked Noddy for all of his commitment and sacrifice.

I looked at Mommy. She was in her wheelchair, not saying a word.

All of the sudden, a feeling of sadness washed over me, and tears began pouring from my eyes. It had just hit me: Noddy, our caregiving foundation, was moving on with his life and I knew that Glen's health would not allow her to duplicate Noddy's involvement. And at that moment, I saw what was about to happen:

We would have to discuss the possibility of putting Mommy in a long-term nursing facility against her will.

I was trying to be the good son, the son who could help lead the family through this tough part of our journey. Remember, I'm the preacher who has counseled many families through this journey. But at that moment, I didn't want to be the Rev. Odell Cleveland. I wanted to be my mother's son, Dell. I just wanted the pain of the recommendation that I knew I was going to suggest – that I felt that I must suggest — to go away. My heart's desire was to make everything OK for Mommy, just like she had made it OK for me and my siblings for so many years. It was hard to accept, but the truth was, I couldn't make it OK — not for me, not for my siblings and not for Mommy.

There were so many worries: What if we select the wrong nursing facility? Will she get the care we'll be paying for? Can we get her in a nursing home in Charleston? How much will it cost each month? What happens if we have to bring her five hours away to Greensboro?

In addition to those concerns, there was my biggest unspoken fear: Will Mommy give up on life and die because we placed her in a facility against her wishes?

At that moment, God reminded me of a conversation that Mommy and I had months ago while she was in bed and I was sitting in her wheelchair. As we talked and laughed about old times, she told me that I was the oldest male in the family and that she was depending on me to make the right decision for the family. I thought she was talking about burial arrangements and making sure that her will was executed as she wished. I was good with that, because those arrangements would be made after she's gone.

But this decision was different. I had to take these actions while looking into my mother's eyes while she was still alive, the same eyes she used 60 years ago to look into her first born son's eyes.

The decision had to be made, and I did it. Through the tears and the guilt, I explained to her how we couldn't take care of her at home anymore and that she had to go to a nursing home.

I still cry every time I think of this conversation, but it's all right. It's OK to cry. I don't even try to hide my tears anymore, because men do cry, and as Mommy used to say, "It's Dell's turn now."

The Bible says that when Solomon became king, he asked God for wisdom (2 Chronicles 1:7-12), and he became the wisest man in the world (1 Kings 4:29-34). In the book of Ecclesiastes, King Solomon wrote about life's experiences:

To everything there is a season, and a time to every purpose under the heaven:

> A time to be born, and a time to die; a time to plant, and a time to plunk up that which is planted;
>
> A time to kill, and a time to heal; a time to break down, and a time to build up;
>
> A time to weep, and a time to laugh; a time to mourn, and a time to dance;
>
> A time to cast away stones, and a time to gather stones together; a time to embrace, and a time to refrain from embracing;
>
> A time to get, and a time to lose; a time to keep, and a time to cast away;

A time to rend, and a time to sew; a time to keep silence, and a time to speak;

A time to love, and a time to hate; a time for war, and a time for peace.

– Ecclesiastes 3:1-8

I often reflect on King Solomon's wise words about the "appointed time," "period of time" and "no more time." In this context, "appointed time" means that there will be a season in my life when I will either be a caregiver or in need of a caregiver. When I consider "period of time," I pause and try to remember how many years it has been since I became an official caregiver.

My next thought is, "How long, Lord? How long will my time as a caregiver last?" I'm not complaining. I would just like to know. Some people might view this as selfish; I understand their perspective. Others might attempt to avoid the question instead of accepting the reality: Your time as a caregiver will last until the death of your loved one.

I often ask a question of people who are or have been caregivers. It's a question I also ask myself: "When your time as a caregiver is over, will you feel relieved or guilty, and will you feel guilty for feeling relieved?" The answers reflect many different emotions, but primary caregivers usually respond with "relieved." Most say that they don't feel guilty for feeling relieved, but rather feel freed and excited to get their life back. A dear friend, while caring for his mother, witnessed her health decline daily over the last six months of her life.

"I wanted her to die," he responded when I asked him the question, "but I didn't want her dead."

Let me assure you: This is normal. It's normal to view the responsibility of caring for a loved one as difficult – maybe even unfair, depending on family dynamics. Yes, it's also noble work, important work, unpaid and underestimated work that often goes unrecognized.

Over the last few years, I have talked with dozens of caregivers, many adult children who are feeling the additional stress of caring for their parents while providing for their own families. My neighbor, a licensed nursing home and assisted living administrator for more than 35 years, shared his perspective as a healthcare provider and a son: "There came a time when I did not want to see patients or my mother suffer any longer. Yes, I would miss them. But I knew it was selfish on my part to desire to keep them in the earthly realm."

In 2016, I helped found Caregiver Connect Inc., a nonprofit started out of Mount Zion Baptist Church that partners with agencies such as AARP, UnitedHealthcare, ROS Therapy Systems and others. In 2018, I produced a radio show in Charleston called "Caregiving 101: The Ministry That Cares for Those Who Care for Others."

Those experiences led me to write this book, "It's My Turn Now."

This isn't a step-by-step guide on how to be a caregiver. Instead, I'm inviting you on a journey, providing you with a safe place for open and honest discussion about dealing with your family's current reality. Hopefully, "It's My Turn Now" will encourage you and affirm that you aren't alone in whatever fear, sadness, embarrassment and, yes, even anger you're feeling.

The world of caregiving can be very hard. It's my fondest wish that "It's My Turn Now" will soften the edges.

CHAPTER 1
WHAT HAPPENED TO MY LIFE?

"What happened to my life, Odell?

"We were supposed to be retired, traveling and enjoying our golden years together. Instead of changing my grandchildren's poopy diapers, I'm changing my husband's poopy diapers. For years, I've anticipated learning foreign languages and new skills, not something called Basic ADLs, the six routine activities people do every day without assistance. What happened to my life?"

The question came from a woman who had been taking care of her husband, but it just as easily could have been posed by any long-term caregiver. Most of us will, at some point in our lives, care for a spouse, partner, parent, grandparent, sibling or some other relation.

Each situation brings its own challenges. A man caring for his wife of 60 years, for example, might find himself cooking, cleaning and washing the clothes for the first time in his life — in addition to his caretaking duties. Or a man with young children might feel guilty about how much time he devotes to his sick father, leaving most of the child care to his wife. Or a woman might have to turn down the promotion of a lifetime because she can't move away from the elderly aunt for whom she cares.

Despite the individual nature of caregiving, there are some universal experiences that unite anyone who has ever served in that role. There's loneliness, compounded by feeling trapped in a circumstance not of your own making. As a caregiver, you aren't in prison, but you are handcuffed. You're shackled. You're taking care of Mom, Dad, a loved one, and right now, for this period of time in your life, you're constrained.

There's also sadness — not just over the loved one's illness, but your loss of freedom as well. Then there's impatience, as the caregiver wonders how long he or she will be fulfilling this obligation. There might even be resentment of other family members who are able but unwilling to help. And finally, there's guilt, something caregivers often feel when they find themselves resenting what they're giving up.

As a minister, I've counseled hundreds of caregivers who have experienced this swirling cycle of emotions. But I've also experienced them myself as I've cared for Mommy along with my older sister and younger brother. And just like you, I've found myself asking, "What happened to my life?"

I grew up in Charleston, S.C., in what we used to call "the projects" off East Bay Street behind Ansonborough Square. Mommy, a divorced mother to the four of us, would work all day as a sewing machine operator at Manhattan Shirt Factory, then attend night school to finish her GED. Luckily, we lived in what would now be called a "walkable community." We had a nice little routine worked out for getting around in our neighborhood while Mommy put food on our table and knowledge in her head. My oldest sister and I would walk to Buist Elementary School (now Buist Academy). It's directly across the street from Emanuel African Methodist Episcopal Church, or "Mother Emanuel," site of a horrible mass shooting in 2015 that took nine beautiful souls. And we would walk across Marion Square, which locals called "the green," to the old Charleston Library.

Everything changed on Feb. 10, 1968. I was seven years old. Mommy told us she wasn't feeling well. She asked my sister Glen to bite her fingers. Glen did — and Mommy couldn't feel it.

She was having a massive stroke.

We called my grandparents, who rushed Mommy to the Medical University of South Carolina, about two miles away. The doctor on duty did a quick assessment of her and said: "You are just experiencing paralysis. You need to come back on free clinic day."

Think about what we now know: Minutes matter for stroke patients. The quicker you receive treatment, the quicker you recover. My sweet, hard-working mother was having a massive stroke, and they sent her home. Why didn't the emergency room physician admit Mommy to the region's best hospital? Mommy had a job. She had insurance. But this was the late 1960s in Charleston.

It took my grandparents another 24 hours — maybe closer to 48 — before finding a Jewish doctor who insisted, ironically to the same physician who originally turned her away, that they admit Mommy to the hospital.

She stayed there for about 2½ months. Everyone thought she was going to die. This was a family crisis. Mommy and her four children, from 18 months to 9 years old, were at the epicenter of the crisis.

Family members would talk, and I always was prone to eavesdropping as a kid. I'd hear them whisper: "What are we going to do with the four children?"

An uncle and his wife were willing to take my baby sister, Sonja Renee Cleveland, a beautiful 18-month-old with hazel eyes. An aunt was willing to take Glen and Noddy — Glenda's "good, well-behaved children."

"Who is going to take Odell?"

I remember feeling sad, scared and alone, wondering why no one in my family seemed to want me.

To hear Mommy tell it, she was having her own conversation as her relatives planned for our futures. Mommy was talking — no, pleading with God.

"God," she prayed, "please allow me to live long enough to see my children grown."

Now, I could go back and talk about the 24 to 48 hours when the hospital didn't take care of my mother. I could ask God: "Why couldn't Mommy have been admitted in the hospital sooner? How might her life — how might MY life and my siblings' lives — have been different had she gotten care earlier?"

But I choose, instead, to say: "God, thank You for listening to Mommy. Thank You for allowing her to live. Thank You for letting her be there for us."

I won't sugarcoat it. None of us had it easy from that point on.

Not my grandparents and my youngest aunt, who took in the five of us at their 1,244-square-foot home at 928 Sycamore Ave. in a part of Charleston called Ashleyville.

Not my siblings and me, who have spent the rest of our lives caring for Mommy in some manner.

And least of all not Mommy, who fought like a warrior for every piece of independence she gained. She relearned to talk, to walk, to drive. During her recovery, her fingers and hands on her left side started closing – a common malady for stroke victims. The doctor asked my siblings and me to help her exercise her hand with a little rubber ball. I remember working with her, urging her, believing that her hand was going to get better because she believed it would.

Mommy never fully healed. Today, she struggles not only with the stroke's permanent and debilitating effects, but with typical illnesses associated with growing older. She can barely walk, is prone to falling, and spends most of her time in a wheelchair. Periodically, she's in significant pain and suffers from memory loss, and she has stage IV breast cancer.

Her issues are constant and relentless. Mommy has good days, and she has bad days.

Sometimes, I embrace my role as caregiver and thank God for the opportunity to help take care of her. Other times, I feel like I'm stuck in a pit. I'm just being honest. I can do that, though it took me a while to get here.

While my struggles pale in comparison to Mommy's, they are real. I live near Greensboro, N.C., five hours away from her, and I don't get home as often as I would like. Many days, I feel as though I should abandon my career and move home to become Mommy's full-time caregiver. But I have a wife. And she has a fulfilling career. Together, we have financial obligations to fulfill as we move toward retirement.

Some days, I imagine moving Mommy to North Carolina to a nursing home where she can get full-time care. I imagine lying to her and to myself, saying I'll visit every day, instead of telling the truth, which is that I'll visit when I can. I imagine Mommy being five hours away from everyone and everything that's familiar to her – church, grandchildren, extended family and friends. I imagine my brother and sister fighting the move, knowing that without sibling buy-in, nothing will work long-term.

Just like Mommy, I have good days, and I have bad days.

Let's revisit the question posed to me from the woman caring for her husband: "What happened to my life?" She's still living her life. I'm still living my life. And you are still living your life. As caregivers, we're going through a stressful, unexpected and even unwanted season. But it's real, not a dress rehearsal.

In the Preface, we discussed King Solomon's insight about "appointed time," "period of time" and "no more time." And we considered his famous passage from Ecclesiastes: "To everything there is a season, and a time to every purpose under heaven."

So I ask you to remember King Solomon's words of wisdom the next time you find yourself asking, "What happened to my life?"

And remember: This, too, shall pass.

CHAPTER 2
THE EPIC STRUGGLE

I was home visiting Mommy not too long ago when – how should I say this politely? — she made her frustrations known about not being able to drive any more.

"Listen," she said to me. "I have to depend on people now. I can't just go get my hair done. I can't just go to the store. I've got to depend on you all" — meaning my brother, sister and me.

"And sometimes," she continued, "y'all get on my last nerve. I'll want you to do something for me, or take me somewhere, and you'll say, 'Well, Mommy, I don't know.' What do you mean, you don't know? I had my own car for years! Dell, I'm the one who taught you how to drive!"

I found myself thinking: "Oh, goodness! I'm a 60-year-old man! Is she going to send me to my room without my supper?"

Remember the person who taught you to drive? Perhaps the time has come for that person to retire from driving for health reasons, but he or she might need some time to adjust to the idea. Because when you take away the car keys from your mother or father, you've taken away their independence.

And that hurts.

Independence is simple. It's freedom from control, influence, support and, yes, help from others. It's an awkward start of the reversal of roles within the family — where the parent becomes the child and the child becomes the parent. When you're talking to someone who wants his or her independence, and you're the one saying no, that's where the issues start.

For many caregivers, driving is the first battle in this epic struggle.

Let's think about it from our point of view – the caregiver's point of view. Driving ability isn't determined by age, but rather by the driver's physical health and mental status. Sometimes, medication affects that. And you know, for example, that when Dad takes a certain medication, his vision is impaired. So you're sitting at home, imagining him driving at night or in the rain, not being able to see clearly, and having an accident. You're terrified by this thought. "God," you cry in your prayers, "I'm responsible for taking care of Dad. How can I protect him from himself? How do I tell him he's a danger to himself and others on the roads?"

Somehow, you summon the courage to broach the subject: "Dad, you know the side effects of that medication," you tell him. "You know that you can't see the way you used to see. How about you give me the car keys? I'll take you where you need to go."

Now let's look at it from another perspective: the perspective of your loved one. Losing the ability to drive – to get in their car and go where they please – is traumatic. Dad wants to go to the store. Mom wants to visit friends. Grandma wants to attend Sunday school. And you've just told them they can't do those things without depending on the help of another human being.

People don't want to be controlled. They want to be in control. So it's not unusual that the person receiving care wants to have as much independence as possible. Which is why aging parents rarely agree with their adult children about driving even when they know it's time to hand over the keys. They will tell you, "Hey, that car is in my name. You have no right to keep me from getting behind the wheel."

Look, I'll be the first to admit how hard it was to take Mommy's car keys. My brother, sister and I had a very pleasant conversation with her as one little fender-bender led to another little fender-bender. Her front and rear bumpers had streaks of various paint colors resulting from scraping cars in the parking lot.

That very pleasant conversation continued for about a year before she actually stopped driving.

Driving is just one part of the epic struggle. As a minister, I visit a lot of families. I love seeing the elderly husband and wife who are taking care of each other. He might not be able to hear well. She might not be able to see well. Yet they've adjusted. They're caring for each other because they wouldn't have it any other way.

However, I've seen this expression of pure love and devotion get to the point where it wears both of them down. What do you do as their adult child? You know that they're fighting for their independence as a couple. You know that their codependency is keeping them alive. You want to allow them to live and love and have some sense of independence, some sense of control. But you live in fear that by allowing that to continue, you're putting their health and safety in grave danger.

There are so many issues you must consider as a caregiver, issues your loved one may see as a challenge to his or her independence. Is it time to pay someone to clean his house? Should you hire a nurse to stay with her overnight? Should we consider moving her to an assisted living center or a nursing home or a relative's house?

How do we, as caregivers, balance their need for independence with our obligation to keep them safe?

First, remember that every discussion with Mom or Dad about giving up another piece of their independence shouldn't be a war. Sometimes, the aim should be redistributing power – in other words, getting your loved one to acknowledge that you now are a partner in his or her decision-making. As caregivers, we don't want to have an all-out war with our loved ones based on their need to be independent.

Also, let the person you're caring for have as much say as possible about important decisions. Give Mom or Dad the easy win whenever possible — without jeopardizing their health.

Finally, work in tandem with other family members or even longtime family friends. There's strength in numbers. Your elderly parents might be more agreeable to handing over the car keys or agreeing to the services of a home health agency if multiple people they love and respect tell them that the time has come.

During a later visit, I said, "Mommy, did you hear that 97-year-old Prince Philip (husband of Queen Elizabeth II) crashed his armored car and handed over his driver licence?"

She looked at me with that contagious smile and said, "Yeah, but I bet he didn't give up all of his sets of keys. Remember, you don't need your driver's license to drive. You need keys."

We both just laughed.

Remember, the person who taught you to drive might need time to adjust to this change in his or her life. Give them the understanding they need.

CHAPTER 3
SIBLING RIVALRY

Twenty-three percent of Americans with children have just one.

The other 77 percent are all too familiar with the topic at hand: sibling rivalry. We spend our first 18 years competing with our siblings for material things (toys, desserts, sports equipment) and for less tangible things (group control, attention from our parents, love). Sibling rivalry often takes the form of teasing, bullying and yelling. It can graduate to mild shoving and hitting.

It's a normal and natural part of every family.

But who are we kidding here? For many families, those old tensions extend into adulthood due to unresolved issues from childhood or new conflicts that emerge later in life. Sometimes, disagreements between siblings can become so severe — and the relationships so broken — that it disrupts caregiving, further complicating an already stressful situation. And it's nearly impossible for siblings with lingering hostilities to work together to care for Mom or Dad, much less peacefully resolve their legal and financial affairs.

Every family dynamic is different. But in my role as pastor, I've noticed a few common conflicts among sibling-caregivers, and I've offered countless families strategies for overcoming those conflicts. Here are a few that might help your family:

THINK EQUAL SACRIFICE, NOT EQUAL GIVING

Siblings share DNA. But they often lead vastly different lives, with different educational backgrounds, different family situations, different income levels. One daughter might have a demanding career. Another might not have a job. A son might travel regularly for work. Another might live next door to Mom or Dad's house and rarely leave town.

So how do sibling-caregivers determine a fair distribution of responsibilities when what they can offer is so dissimilar? Does it mean equal giving, where everyone contributes exactly the same amount of time, money and energy to take care of their loved one, regardless of their circumstances? Or does it mean equal sacrifice, with each child doing what they can when they can?

Think back to when you were little, and your mom would bring home a dozen doughnuts. You and your siblings couldn't do the math fast enough. You would immediately divide 12 by the number of people in your household to arrive at how many of those doughnuts were yours. Remember when your little sister got to go on her first movie date at age 14, something you weren't allowed to do until you were 16? You stomped your feet and screamed, "That's not fair!"

You can't do that with caregiving. You can't expect that every task, every responsibility will be divided up equally — fair or not.

My big sister, younger brother and I work well together on Mommy's care. We deal with the situation through equal sacrifice, not equal giving. We divvy up those sacrifices of time, money and energy as best we can, remembering that the amounts we can offer might vary over time depending on where we are in our lives. We don't keep score of who gives what, but we try to sacrifice equally.

And we remind each other that we want the same thing: what's best for Mommy.

DON'T BE A MARTYR

Primary caregivers sometimes feel as though their siblings have abandoned them.

Maybe your brother calls Dad once a week, something that brightens Dad's day. Maybe your sister sends money regularly to ease Mom's financial burden. All of that is wonderful. But each time the phone rings and each time a check arrives in the mail, you think: "Brother, Sister, when are you coming home? When is it your turn to spend the night with Mom? When are you going to give me a break?"

And each time, you say nothing.

How long until you reach your limit and lash out at your siblings, who might not realize you're struggling? How long before you've made a federal case out of something that could have been handled with two simple words: "Help me?"

Yes, it's possible that your siblings are shirking their duties. But it's also possible that they're willing to step in and relieve you. You won't know until you ask.

EXERT AUTHORITY WITHOUT VENGEANCE

Let's say Mom has given you her power-of-attorney, which provides you with the authority to act on her behalf in financial and legal matters. You're in charge of her bank accounts, her rental income, her insurance policies, all of her worldly possessions. You'll also handle her estate when she dies.

Let's also say that at some point — perhaps when you were little, perhaps just recently — one of your siblings did you wrong. I mean, really wrong. So wrong that a complete stranger who learned what had happened would say, "Yeah, that was cold."

Now you have all the power. Now you're finally in a position to exact your revenge.

Let's talk about what you do with those feelings, about how you treat your siblings once you have the upper hand.

You may not want to hear my advice: Treat them fairly. Don't reenact their bad behavior by behaving badly. Don't "forget" to let them know about changes in your loved one's condition. Don't punish them by withholding things that are rightfully theirs, like money, property or precious family heirlooms.

Yes, you are in control. But it's not about you. So use your power as a way to get the best possible care for your loved one, not as a tool for revenge.

BE PART OF THE SOLUTION, NOT THE PROBLEM

Lastly, consider your own feelings about your siblings, your own unresolved issues from childhood. It's OK to be honest and say to yourself, "I'm still upset about something that happened 30 or 40 years ago." Maybe you can't yet forgive your brothers and sisters for their transgressions. Maybe you're not ready to move on.

That's OK.

But don't hold up the process of helping your loved one by refusing to work with your siblings, by arguing with them, by engaging in passive-aggressive behavior, by making decisions as if they don't exist. That undermines all the work you're doing to care for your loved one. And from a practical point of view, it will muddy the waters when the time comes to plan the funeral and settle the estate.

When it comes to our brothers and sisters, it's very easy to slip into old familiar patterns. Your instinct is to revert to the child who could bicker, yell or fight their way out of a conflict. Now that you're a caregiver, you no longer have that luxury.

You're the grown-up in the room. And it's your turn now to act like one.

CHAPTER 4
TRUTH AND HARMONY
THE EIGHT KEYS TO RUNNING A PEACEFUL FAMILY MEETING

Everybody wants harmony. Sometimes, truth is more important.

But as a caregiver, you don't have the luxury of valuing one over the other. Not when it comes to dealing with your family.

You must have both.

There will come a point — and maybe you've reached it already — when you recognize that the situation with your loved one has changed and you need to make an adjustment. Perhaps Mom is ready for around-the-clock care. Or Dad has a new medical condition that requires you to make some decisions about his treatment.

This, my friends, is the "appointed time" King Solomon spoke of.

You can't make the decision alone. You may be the primary caregiver, but there are other family members deeply invested in your loved one's care. The situation calls for a family meeting. It's a chance to provide family members with information, receive input from them about how to handle the situation, and gather support for the consequences of the decision.

I know what some of you are thinking: My people don't want to hear the truth. They can't accept the reality that Mom's health is failing, much less take part in the decision-making. Or maybe you're wondering whether you can gather your brothers and sisters together for a meeting about the next steps in Dad's dementia care without it devolving into an hour-long shouting match over decades-old grudges.

Look, families are complicated things, and bringing yours together for a peaceful, productive meeting might seem like an impossible task. But if you don't at least try to unite everyone for a discussion, then you invite misunderstandings and hard feelings. And that's the best-case scenario. Worst-case scenario? Without family meetings, you run the risk of divisions over medical care, fights for control over decision-making or maybe even court actions. None of these scenarios are in your loved one's best interest. And acting in your loved one's best interest is Priority No. 1 for you as the primary caregiver.

You're not the first caregiver in history to get stressed out by the idea of holding a family meeting. I've counseled enough families over the years and attended enough meetings with my own family to offer some advice on how to organize and run a successful and peaceful family meeting:

1. DECIDE WHO SHOULD ATTEND

In many ways, the guest list depends on how your family defines "family." Some people grew up in the two-parent, multiple-child household that many people call "the traditional family." However, there are as many other ways to define "family" as there are families in the world. We live in the era of the "extended family," which might include your loved one's spouse or partner, your step-siblings and their spouses, even aunts, uncles, cousins, close friends or neighbors.

After all, it takes a village. Include those members of your village who have a vested interest in your loved one's situation and who have some standing to participate in decision-making on his or her behalf.

Perhaps you're thinking that the guest list should depend on the discussion topics. Maybe your sister is adamantly opposed to moving Mom into a nursing home, and you'd rather not deal with her opposition to what you know is inevitable. Or maybe your stepmother doesn't want to admit that Dad's chemotherapy is doing him more harm than good, and you don't want her to know that you've asked the doctors to discontinue treatment.

I would recommend against tailoring the guest list based on the discussion topic. Remember, you must strike a balance between truth and harmony. Everyone with a vested interest in your loved one's care deserves to know all of the facts, regardless of whether it makes your situation as primary caregiver more difficult.

2. IF AT ALL POSSIBLE, INVITE YOUR LOVED ONE

Your loved one has a right to attend — if their medical condition makes their participation in a meeting such as this reasonable. They might not agree with the outcome of the meeting, but they'll at least know their voice has been heard.

A while back, I was having a business meeting with a man whose 95-year-old mother had been ill. She had run the entire health-care gamut — from home-health provider to assisted living center to intermediate care to skilled nursing — and was nearing the end of her life. Just one night earlier, he and his brother, along with their wives, held a family meeting and decided to call in hospice.

"Now we've got to tell Momma," he told me with some degree of resignation.

"How are you going to approach it with her?" I asked.

"I'm not sure," he said. "She's going to tell us she doesn't need hospice. Momma doesn't accept a lot of what has happened to her. She believes she's going to live to be 98."

I asked: "Why 98?"

"So she can outlive her aunt," he said.

I suggested a way to broach the subject with Momma: Ask why she wants to outlive her aunt. Invite her into the conversation that way — rather than telling her what you and your brother are going to do. It might open the door to comparing her health challenges to her aunt's, then discussing why living another three years might not be possible. It also might begin a conversation about how much pain she's willing to endure; whether she wants to remain on life support or be resuscitated; and how she wants to spend her final moments.

It is, after all, Momma's life we're talking about.

"You know," he told me, "I never thought about that."

3. PICK A LOCATION

Choose a spot where most people will feel comfortable, preferably a neutral location that promotes an open discussion. Depending on your family, that might mean meeting in public, perhaps at a coffee shop or restaurant. Or if you feel that privacy is paramount, consider asking for space at a house of worship or a community center.

Try to minimize noise and distraction. If you have young kids, leave them at home. You need to have a place where you can really get into it.

As most of us learned during the coronavirus pandemic, technology assures that everybody can participate in this meeting — whether they live 5,000 miles away or happen to be on vacation. Include them in the meeting by using the telephone, Zoom, Skype, Google Hangout, Facetime or any other communications app. Make arrangements for whatever technology you'll need before the meeting begins to minimize disruptions and maximize time.

4. SET AN AGENDA

Send it to the meeting's participants ahead of time so they'll be prepared to talk about your loved one's issues. Don't shroud it in mystery by saying, "I don't want to say what the meeting's about until we're all together." Nobody wants to be surprised or ambushed by topics they're going to be asked to discuss.

List all the meeting's participants on the agenda, including any roles you have assigned them. Appoint a timekeeper to stick to the specified length; a gatekeeper to ensure discussions stay on topic; and a secretary to record thoughts, concerns and decisions. And because communication can be a challenge even for the highest-functioning families, note on the agenda whether a facilitator or neutral third party will lead the meeting.

Finally, if necessary, use the agenda to set out the rules of engagement: "Participants will use respectful language. Participants will stay on topic. Participants promise not to leave the meeting in anger."

Now, I'm not suggesting that you run this family discussion like a City Council meeting, following Robert's Rules of Order. But an agenda, while business-like, allows you to clearly state the point of the meeting, set expectations for conduct and behavior, and anticipate solutions to conflicts that might jeopardize a successful outcome.

5. ASK QUESTIONS DURING THE MEETING

Don't immediately jump into problem-solving mode. Listen to your fellow meeting-goers, then ask questions to get a better understanding of their opinions about your loved one's care. For instance, you might say to your sister: "I'm not sure I understood your point. Could you say it a different way?" Then she can clarify her statement so it's not misconstrued by you or anyone else at the meeting.

Remember, you're trying to avoid conflict and promote collaboration on behalf of your loved one. Asking questions will make participants feel heard, increasing the likelihood of agreement.

6. STAY ON TOPIC

Every family has a shared history and emotional baggage. Without proper precautions, family meetings can quickly become forums for airing long-standing grievances between relatives.

Don't let unresolved conflicts from 20 years ago derail the original intent of your meeting. Empower the gatekeeper or the person running the meeting to say, if such an issue were to arise, "No. That's not the issue we're dealing with today. We're dealing with the here and now." Remind the meeting's participants of your common goal: finding the best possible solution to a change in your loved one's situation.

7. MAKE AGREEMENTS, ASSIGN RESPONSIBILITIES

Let me be honest: You won't leave this meeting, no matter how well you've planned, with every issue resolved. Your goal should be general agreement and trust rather than a perfect solution.

Make sure you end the meeting with those agreements clearly stated and recorded by the meeting's secretary.

The same goes for assigning responsibilities. Those solutions you've just agreed to? Not every one of them must be done by you. Caregivers have enough pressures — emotional and financial, work and home — without feeling as though they can't ask for help. Say to your family members: "OK, Brother, you're good with the internet. Research the new Medicare options. Sister, you're good with numbers. Go over the doctor bill and make sure we weren't overcharged. Sister-in-law, you know the community. Find a reliable lawn care service to take care of Daddy's yard."

Those assignments should become part of the meeting's minutes, too.

Here's an example from my own family: Ever since I was named Mommy's power-of-attorney, I've felt awkward. It's kind of like one of my favorite sayings: "Unintended consequences are just unanticipated consequences, but consequences just the same." Armed with this awareness, I was constantly looking for ways to make sure my siblings didn't feel negatively about Mommy's decision.

Then I found it. My answer was wrapped in a problem.

During one of our earlier family meetings, Noddy raised the question about writing checks to pay Mommy's bills. He said, "Odell, how are you planning on coming home to sign the checks when needed?" The truth was, I'd never really thought about the day-to-day activities, since Noddy and Glen always handled everything so beautifully.

So I suggested that Noddy and Glen open an additional bank account with both of their names on it. After more discussion, Mommy, my siblings and I agreed to use the additional account to deposit the monthly contributions that my siblings and I make each month to cover Mommy's care.

The arrangement is a good check and balance for everyone involved. But more importantly to me, at least, it's an opportunity to show my siblings that I'm not trying to control everything, that I'm a team player. It might just be in my head, but since that decision, the awkwardness around Mommy granting me her power-of-attorney has gone away.

Mommy's OK with this arrangement, though she sometimes comments about not having control of her own money. Her monthly disability check goes to her original account, which she and my sister manage. To address Mommy's concerns about not having access to her money (which isn't true), I make sure that every time that I come home, I give Mommy a "nice piece of money." Now she no longer experiences the aggravation of having no control over her money. Remember, anything that prevents your loved one from becoming aggravated is welcome.

Don't tell Mommy, but giving her that "nice piece of money" brings me as much joy as it does to her. When I was a child every Friday, she would give us a quarter for our allowance. I loved it, and so did she.

8. DON'T UNDERMINE THE MEETING WITH A POST-MEETING MEETING

I cannot stress this enough: Don't call two of your four siblings after the meeting to say, "Well, I didn't want to say anything in front of the others, but there's another issue going on we need to discuss." Say it all — to everyone — during the meeting, even if you know you won't get 100 percent buy-in. Better to get it out in the open than to create an opportunity for future conflict. You know as well as I do that those other two will find out about that call.

I'll end this chapter by once again acknowledging what we all know: Caregiving is hard. Making decisions about your loved one is hard. Dealing with your family is hard. It might seem like avoiding family meetings about tough subjects is the easiest way out.

It's not. Sometimes, caregiving is hard because we've chosen not to deal with certain issues.

You now have the tools for a successful and peaceful family meeting. So gather everyone around a table for some truth and harmony.

CHAPTER 5

BEING THERE FOR DAD (THOUGH HE WASN'T THERE FOR YOU)

Most men try to be great fathers. They show up for parent-teacher conferences and play catch after long days at work. They make flashcards for multiplication quizzes and pack PB&J sandwiches in lunch bags. And a special few, when no one is looking, sip imaginary tea out of tiny pink cups at a party for stuffed animals.

But some men don't try. At all. They are fathers in name only, passing along the genes, carrying the official title, but not living the life of "Dad." Maybe they were absent from the moment you were born, or left the family when you were little. Maybe they struggled with alcohol or drug abuse, or spent extended periods behind bars. Maybe they dropped in and out of your life, raising your hopes for a healthy, steady relationship, but always letting you down.

Eventually, however, all fathers find themselves in need of care from a loved one, no matter how good or bad their parenting.

That's when "It's My Turn Now" takes on a whole new meaning.

Look, it's hard enough to become the primary caregiver to the best dad in the world — Parent-Teacher Conference Dad, Flashcard Dad, Tea Party Dad. But what about a stranger, or worse, someone who was neglectful or abusive? How do you decide whether to sacrifice your time, your job security, your relationships with others and fully devote yourself to a man who wasn't there for you when you needed him most?

Unfortunately, I've seen many examples of this type of situation through my ministerial duties. I've counseled countless people as they agonized over how much care to provide an absentee parent — most often a father, but occasionally a mother — who was terminally ill and had nowhere else to turn.

And it's never as simple as, "Yes, I will take care of him," or, "No, I won't take care of her."

First and foremost, you have to stop for a moment and feel your own feelings — about the past, about the present, about all of it — before deciding whether to take on the role as caregiver to this person. That means acknowledging anger, hurt, resentment, grief or disappointment when it arises.

You might experience more complicated emotions as well.

Relief: "I finally have a chance to repair my relationship with Dad before he dies."

Guilt: "Maybe I should have done more to reach out to him as he has gotten older."

Jealousy: "He spent all those years raising his stepchildren, so why am I the one stuck taking care of him?"

Indifference: "I'm sorry that Dad isn't well, but it's not my problem."

And don't forget confusion. You're going to go back and forth about what to do — to care or not to care. The Bible makes caring for our parents a moral and spiritual imperative. God had the option of handing down thousands of commandments to Moses, but instead He went with the most important ones. "Honor thy father and thy mother" made the Top 10 list.

But do we honor those who aren't honorable? Do we honor those who abandoned us?

Do we honor abuse?

These questions don't have easy answers.

Then there are further complications to consider: How might your decision affect other family members? Imagine telling your mother that you're suddenly the primary caregiver for a man who, 40 years earlier, left his whole family for another woman. When you look at your father, you see a sick, elderly man who needs you. But when your mother looks at him, she sees the young, healthy man who deserted his family.

In that situation, are you betraying your mother to care for your father?

Your decision also impacts your siblings. Let's say you choose not to join your brothers and sisters in caring for your ailing father because the past is still too painful for you. They might pressure you to help them. "You're being too sensitive," they might tell you. "Let bygones be bygones," they might say.

My advice? Gently remind them that we all heal at our own pace. And you're not there yet.

On the other hand, you might find yourself resenting your family for forgiving him. You angrily ask your siblings: "How can you take care of him after what he did to us? After what he did to Mom?"

Here's the reality: Your brothers and sisters have the right to help their father, just as you have the right not to. Healing doesn't follow a timeline.

Finally, before deciding whether to step into the role as caregiver, you must consider the emotional, psychological and, yes, financial state of the parent who has returned to your life and is asking for your help.

As you know, I'm a Baptist minister. In my faith tradition, we believe that one can become a new man (or woman) in Jesus Christ. We believe He will wash away the sins of the past — symbolized by our baptism ritual — and provide a new path toward salvation.

As folks in the South might say, "Dad's done been saved."

So now what? Jesus Christ Himself, Lord of all, has forgiven your father. And you're not going to?

You might be ready to forgive. But that doesn't mean you have to forget. You don't have to forget the hurt, the struggle, the feelings of abandonment you've been carrying around for the last 40 years. In fact, it's probably better that you do remember the past — for your own protection.

I'll never forget the story a member of my church told me. We had recently discovered that we were both caring for a parent, and we'd just begun sharing experiences with each other.

"You know, Odell," he told me, "Dad asked for my help after all those years of not being in my life. He asked me to take care of him and take over financial responsibility of his properties, pay his taxes, his bills and everything."

I asked: "So how did you handle it?"

"I said, 'OK, Dad, I will help you. But you need to put a few of these properties in my name if I'm going to take on the financial responsibility.'"

"That seems reasonable," I said.

"Dad said, 'No, no, we're not going to do that. I don't want your mother getting it.'"

Then my friend became animated, as though he were talking directly to his father: "But why wouldn't we do that? You're asking me to take on the burden, take over the financial responsibility of the life you led without me. And that's fine. I'll do it. But, Dad, you don't have a will. So if I am going to do this, then I am asking you to let me get your financial stuff in order so I'm not stuck with a mess after you're gone."

I was hanging on his every word: "What did he say?" I asked eagerly.

"He said, 'No. I won't do it.'"

My friend continued: "And that's when I told him: 'Dad, I can't allow you to use me. I'm here. I love you. I want to reconcile. But it's a two-way street. Partnership means love has to go both ways. I understand the issues you had with Mom. But we're not talking about Mom now. We are talking about our relationship. You and me, not as a man to a boy, but as two adults — man to man. Dad, we're going to do this thing, but we're going to do it a certain way. Or we are not going to do it at all.'"

So how did they resolve it? The father transferred some properties to his son's name. And the son became his caregiver.

In the end, when you're facing the decision about caring for a parent who didn't care for you, you have to be like my friend. You have to make the decision that's best for you — on your terms. Some people, including family and close friends, might not understand your decision. That's fine. They don't have to understand it, and you don't have to justify it.

The most important thing, though, is that you think it through carefully — prayerfully, if you're a person of faith. Because you'll likely live with the ramifications of your decision for years to come.

CHAPTER 6
THE HOSPITAL

One of your roles as caregiver is explainer-in-chief.

Never is this more true than when your loved one is in the hospital. You're the person getting all the information. The doctor comes in to talk to you. The nurse comes in to talk to you. You're listening to the dietitian, the physical therapist, the phlebotomist.

So it stands to reason that you're the person giving out all the information. You're summarizing the diagnosis, the treatment, the medical terminology for family and friends. You're providing updates over and over — every time the phone rings or the text alert dings. You're fielding questions from well-meaning relatives: "Did you ask the doctor this? What did the nurse say about that? Why won't they hurry up and run the test? If it were me, I'd take him to another hospital."

You're even expected to tell visitors how to get to the room.

There's no rest for the weary. And definitely no rest in a hospital. Not for the patient. Not for the caregiver.

I know you're not complaining, though it would be understandable if you did. It's overwhelming. Sometimes, you just want to scream, "Listen, I'm doing the best I can!" As a caregiver, the pressure hits when your loved one is suffering, when they call in hospice, when the doctors say, "We've done all we can."

Sometimes, good news can be overwhelming, too — such as when your loved one is ready to leave the hospital and return home. You're ready to celebrate ... until you realize that home might not be ready for them.

When Mommy was first released, we weren't prepared.

Many years after her stroke, Mommy had to be hospitalized after a fall. When she was released, she entered a rehabilitation center.

She thrived there. When her insurance benefits were about to be exhausted, an administrator told us that she was going to be released within two weeks. Her physical condition was greatly diminished, and she was still receiving monthly chemotherapy injections. This triggered a frantic search for a new place for Mommy. We weren't successful. Instead, we cobbled together a care plan and Mommy returned to her home. Thankfully, the plan worked.

Regardless of where your loved one goes when they leave — to their home or your home, a skilled nursing unit or to heaven — their time in the hospital will have a lasting impact on you, the caregiver. You will be the one who asks hard questions of the doctor. You will be the one reviewing the bills and dealing with the insurance company. You will make decisions about post-hospital care plans and living arrangements.

In Chapter 4, "Truth and Harmony," we discussed ways to hold a successful, peaceful family meeting. I recommend that you have one during your loved one's hospital stay and another once the hospitalization has ended. Remember that the goal of these meetings is general agreement, not a perfect solution. Sometimes, you walk away not with a win-win but with an OK-OK.

And do yourself a favor: If at all possible, use the meeting to delegate some of your tasks to other family members, such as reviewing the hospital bill or collecting your loved one's belongings. That will allow you to spend the majority of your time providing care.

After all, explainer-in-chief isn't a title you want to keep forever.

CHAPTER 7
WHEN THINGS FALL APART: THE SERENITY PRAYER

One of the most popular affirmations today is the Serenity Prayer, which was written in the 1930s by the American theologian Reinhold Niebuhr.

In 1940, Alcoholics Anonymous began using a shortened version in its 12-step program: "God, grant me the serenity to accept the things I cannot change, courage to change the things I can, and wisdom to know the difference."

Niebuhr's full prayer, however, goes like this:

God, give me grace to accept with serenity

the things that cannot be changed,

Courage to change the things

which should be changed,

and the wisdom to distinguish

the one from the other.

Living one day at a time,

Enjoying one moment at a time,

Accepting hardship as a pathway to peace,

Taking, as Jesus did,

This sinful world as it is,

Not as I would have it,

Trusting that You will make all things right,

If I surrender to Your will,

So that I may be reasonably happy in this life,

And supremely happy with You forever in the next.

Amen.

Caregivers, does that speak to you?

Research shows the health impact — both mental and physical — of your role as caregiver. Sometimes, it clashes with your full-time job and your boss doesn't like it. Sometimes, you're lonely because you no longer have access to the same social life as before.

Sometimes, you're dead tired from all the feeding, bathing, driving, nursing and bill paying you're doing for someone else.

You are the person in charge. You deal with the house, the taxes, the cars. You deal with the medical insurance, the hospital bills, the long-term care negotiations.

You deal with your family's truths and your family's lies.

At some point, you're bound to break down. It happens.

"Listen to me," you cry — maybe to your family members, maybe in private. "Everybody's asking about how Mother is doing. How Dad is doing. Who's asking about me? Who's caring about the caregiver? I have a family, too. I need help. I need understanding. I need other people."

Yes, you do. But even more than that, you need the acceptance, the courage and the wisdom to deal with your life as a caregiver.

It's the key to living one day at a time, enjoying one moment at a time and accepting hardship as the pathway to peace.

***

'ACCEPT THE THINGS I CANNOT CHANGE'

One day, we had what I like to call a "situation" at Mommy's house in Maryville.

"Odell, the tree fell down," Noddy, who lives with Mommy, said over the phone.

I knew immediately the tree he was talking about: the big one. The one we played under as kids. The one we carved our initials into. And now, that grand old tree was down. It crushed our fence. It tore up the neighbor's fence, blocked traffic and took down power lines. It damaged another neighbor's fence across the street. It damaged Noddy's truck and boat that were parked along the street. That's how big this tree was.

So we called 911. The fire department arrived, then the power company, then Urban Forestry with their chainsaws. Part of the tree remained upright but weakened, so we had to make sure it didn't fall into the neighbor's yard. All the while, family members were taking pictures, calling the insurance company, reading policies, scheduling an adjuster.

There's a word for this: chaos. As one of Mommy's caregivers, I had a plan. My siblings and I had a routine involving her care. And that tree falling? Not part of the plan. Not part of the routine. It was something else for us to handle. Something else to fix. And more pressure on all of us.

Yes, there are some things that you, as a caregiver, can control: How frequently we communicate with family members. Where our loved one receives medical care. How much financial, emotional and social sacrifice we're willing to make to become a caregiver.

But what about the things we can't control?

What do we do, as caregivers, when things fall apart? What happens when the unexpected happens? How do we react when we're given one more thing to deal with — at a point when we've long since reached our limit?

"God," I have prayed on more than one occasion (maybe even the one with the tree), "grant me serenity!"

We must learn that we can't control everything. Sometimes, problems arise that are external — meaning we didn't cause them. We were just minding our own business when something outside of our control happened. The tree that fell at Mommy's is a perfect example. Nobody caused that tree to fall. Call it an act of God. But my family had to deal with it.

I understand why, as caregivers, we fight to keep everything under our control. We're used to picking up the pieces when things fall apart. It's a lot to ask someone — this business of taking responsibility for things we can't control.

It'll be a little easier to cope if you remind yourself that the crisis is temporary — like the tree at Mommy's house. The workers cleared the road. The electric company restored power. The insurance paid for damages to the neighbor's fence and the house across the street.

It was a huge inconvenience to my brother, my sister and me, but we got through it. And now it's over, and we'll never have to deal with it again.

You might be thinking, "I know, Odell. I know I shouldn't worry about things I can't control, but I can't help it. My mind just won't turn off."

Caregivers, you must learn to accept the things you cannot change — for the sanity of your loved one, your family ... and you. We encounter no harder lesson on our caregiving journeys.

But once we do learn the lesson, we begin, as Niebuhr promised, to accept "hardship as a pathway to peace."

***

'COURAGE TO CHANGE THE THINGS I CAN'

There is plenty, however, that we can control in the course of providing care to our loved ones, patterns of behavior and actions that we *can* change.

For instance, you can control your internal reaction to external forces. And by that I mean — letting people live rent-free in our minds.

We have a lot of quiet moments — what I like to call "thinking moments" — when if we're not careful, our thoughts will lead us to destinations we didn't intend to go. Sometimes, our thinking can get complicated, like when other people put thoughts in our heads. How many times, caregiver, have you been doing OK until somebody comes along and says: "You should never have paid that bill. You let the doctor rip us off."

Or, "I'd never let my mom walk all over me like your mother does."

Or, "How can you live with yourself, putting Aunt Judy in a nursing home?"

Folks, these thoughts can cause things to fall apart. With you. Inside.

Occasionally, other people will challenge the job you're doing as caregiver even as you're doing the absolute best you can. It will be particularly hurtful if the criticism comes from a family member.

When this happens, there are two scenarios to consider.

The first — and this might be hard to accept — is that your family member is right. Maybe you should hear what your family member is saying, even if he or she is saying it in an unkind manner. Maybe you *should have* asked for help reviewing the doctor bill. Maybe you do need to stand up to your mother. Maybe it was too soon to move Aunt Judy out of her home.

If that's the case, then summon the "courage to change the things (you) can."

The second scenario is more common, though. It's likely that those disapproving words are all talk. Your critic doesn't want your job. The truth is, most people don't want to do what you're doing. In fact, they don't have the emotional fortitude to last one day caring for your shared loved one.

Niebuhr reminds us in "Serenity Prayer" that all of us must take "this sinful world as it is, not as (we) would have it." I think he means we don't have to be perfect. We have to accept that we won't be perfect caregivers, and so do our loved ones — especially those who are evaluating us from afar.

Don't let their "stinkin' thinkin'" — to borrow another phrase from our friends at Alcoholics Anonymous — make things fall apart.

***

'WISDOM TO KNOW THE DIFFERENCE'

I often talk with family caregivers who are on the front row. They don't want to be on the front row, but there they are. They witness the sights and sounds — sometimes the fights and sounds — of the routine and the unexpected.

Many times during our counseling, I realize that they're struggling to accept the things they cannot change —that their loved one is ill, that this is their appointed time to be a caregiver, that their life is about to change drastically. They don't want these things to be true, so they live in denial.

And I also talk to some folks who aren't willing to change the things they can control. Their family lacks a unified caregiving plan, yet they won't hold a family meeting. Or they don't know their loved one's preferences for end-of-life care, and they're reluctant to broach the subject.

These problems, although difficult, are solvable — if they're willing to have some uncomfortable but necessary conversations.

You can't prevent health challenges, but you can make sure that doctor appointments are made and kept, that prescriptions are filled, that medications are taken as directed by the doctor. During tough days, always try to maintain a positive attitude, remembering that this situation isn't good for them, either.

There's also what Niebuhr called "the wisdom to know the difference" — in other words, knowing what you can control and what you can't.

An example might be your ongoing struggle to convince a sibling to help out more with a parent. You can ask your brother or sister for assistance, and maybe even apply a little guilt. No matter how hard you try, you can't force a person to do something he or she doesn't want to do. In these instances, it's best to use acceptance as your coping mechanism: "I wish I were getting more help from my brother (or sister). However, the fact is I can't count on that, and I have to turn to other sources for assistance."

Too often, caregivers waste their (very limited) energy trying to change the behavior of others. You can call it persistence — or stubbornness — but it's really a refusal to accept that you cannot control anyone but yourself. Remember what Niebuhr said: You have to take "the world as it is, not as I would have it."

Caregivers, you must learn to discern which situations call for acceptance and which call for change.

You must develop "the wisdom to distinguish the one from the other."

CHAPTER 8

THE PRODIGAL SON (OR DAUGHTER) RETURNS

Here's a situation that might sound familiar:

Your sibling left home after high school and didn't come back — rarely calling home, much less stopping in to visit Mom or Dad. And when your parent grew old and infirm, you were the one left behind to provide care. Day in and day out.

You did it all: Driving to doctor visits. Arranging the finances. Cooking, cleaning, even pulling bedpan duty. All the waiting, all the worrying, all the decision-making rested on your shoulders.

Meanwhile, your wayward sibling seemed to be having a good old time — at least based on the Facebook posts that documented weekend getaways, dinners out with friends, even frequent naps. Your brother or sister looked five years younger every time you went online — which admittedly wasn't very often because of how you were running yourself ragged as a caregiver.

And when your sibling finally returned home, yearning for the comfort of family, embarrassed by how long they had neglected Mom or Dad?

Everyone was thrilled, especially your ailing parent.

Everyone except you. You were angry, resentful and a little jealous.

If this story rings a bell, it's because it sounds pretty similar to one of the most famous parables from the Bible: the story of the prodigal son. In Luke 15, Jesus talks about a man with two sons:

> 12 The younger one said to his father, "Father, give me my share of the estate. So he divided his property between them. 13 Not long after that, the younger son got together all he had, set off for a distant country and there squandered his wealth in wild living.

> 14 After he had spent everything, there was a severe famine in that whole country, and he began to be in need. 15 So he went and hired himself out to a citizen of that country, who sent him to his fields to feed pigs. 16 He longed to fill his stomach with the pods that the pigs were eating, but no one gave him anything.

> 17 When he came to his senses, he said, "How many of my father's hired servants have food to spare, and here I am starving to death! 18 I will set out and go back to my father and say to him: Father, I have sinned against heaven and against you. 19 I am no longer worthy to be called your son; make me like one of your hired servants."

20 So he got up and went to his father. But while he was still a long way off, his father saw him and was filled with compassion for him; he ran to his son, threw his arms around him and kissed him.

21 The son said to him, "Father, I have sinned against heaven and against you. I am no longer worthy to be called your son."

22 But the father said to his servants, "Quick! Bring the best robe and put it on him. Put a ring on his finger and sandals on his feet. 23 Bring the fattened calf and kill it. Let's have a feast and celebrate. 24 For this son of mine was dead and is alive again; he was lost and is found." So they began to celebrate.

25 Meanwhile, the older son was in the field. When he came near the house, he heard music and dancing. 26 So he called one of the servants and asked him what was going on. 27 "Your brother has come," he replied, "and your father has killed the fattened calf because he has him back safe and sound."

28 The older brother became angry and refused to go in. So his father went out and pleaded with him. 29 But he answered his father, "Look! All these years I've been slaving for you and never disobeyed your orders. Yet you never gave me even a young goat so I could celebrate with my friends. 30 But when this son of yours who has squandered your property with prostitutes comes home, you kill the fattened calf for him!"

Most of you can understand the way the older brother felt. On a good day, caregiving is emotionally and physically draining. We become frustrated, even angry. We feel guilty, thinking we should do more for our loved one. We get lonely, knowing that we don't have the free time we once had to socialize.

And, of course, we're exhausted. Always exhausted.

So imagine the older brother rolling up from a hard day's work and finding himself in the middle of a big party.

"Hey, your little brother came back," one of the servants tells him.

My brother? The one who took his money and left? My no-good brother? The one who turned his back on the family? That's who we're celebrating? I've been here all this time and nobody has ever celebrated me."

Some of you can relate. Others have smaller versions of the "prodigal son" experience. You know, the brother whose quick visit to the nursing home makes Mom's day. Or the sister who drops in on her way home from church. They make 30 minutes worth of small talk, then stand up and say, "Well, I gotta go now." And your parents? They're happy for the rest of the day, just because that person called.

And you say to yourself, "What about me? I've been here the whole time!"

Here's my question: Caregivers, why does this bother you so much? Why are you bitter that Mom or Dad is happy to hear from another sibling who, in your mind, doesn't do enough?

It's because you see it as an injustice. Here you are doing all the work — and someone else gets the party.

This is a very normal, very human feeling. There's even a word for it: martyrdom.

But there's something important you must remember: It's not about you. It's about your mom or dad. Her happiness. His happiness. We should be celebrating for them when the prodigal son (or daughter) returns. Let's love it for the one we are caring for because they love it.

You should also remember this: Your loved one knows exactly what is going on. He or she recognizes how hard you've been working —

and more importantly, how your Herculean effort compares to the actions of your wayward sibling.

A man I was counseling told me something that bears out my theory. When the man's father was on his deathbed, he called his son close and said: "I'm going to leave you in charge of everything. But let me tell you what's going to happen the minute I close my eyes." And the man said that his father predicted — with pinpoint accuracy, it turns out — how all of his children were going to act when he died. Then the father told his son how to handle their demands.

Parents know. The father in Jesus's parable knew. In Luke 15:31-32, he tells his older son "you are always with me, and everything I have is yours. But we had to celebrate and be glad, because this brother of yours was dead and is alive again; he was lost and is found."

The father had compassion for the prodigal son. The father forgave him.

And so should we.

***

In the Bible, the prodigal son came home a changed man. Humble. Remorseful. Repentant.

In the real world, that's not always how they return.

Some family members never have that moment of clarity when they regret their past decisions and work to make amends with their loved ones. They just keep getting themselves into trouble, keep asking you to bail them out — metaphorically and, in some cases, literally.

Now that person expects you, the responsible caregiver, to comply with his demands. Because that's what your shared loved one — the person for whom you are now caring — would have done. Mom would have sent him money to pay overdue credit card bills. Or Dad would have found him a new place to live when he got kicked out of the last apartment. But you make the decisions these days, so that person comes to you.

Always you.

Your relative occasionally calls or emails you, always under the guise of checking on your loved one. "What's going on with Mom?" Or, "What did the doctor say about Dad?" You know, however, that he's really working you, priming the pump, greasing the wheels to ask for whatever he needs this time. You are standing between that person and what he wants.

What do you do?

It's simple: Don't let that person add to your workload. That may sound harsh, but as a caregiver, you only have so much bandwidth. You must prioritize your time, your talents, your energy and yes, your loved one's money. Bottom line? Your relative is just adding to your workload.

"I know Mom gave you money," you should tell them. "But I'm not Mom."

"I know Dad co-signed your car loan," you should say. "But I'm not Dad."

Saying "no" to a family member, especially a sibling, can be even more difficult when that person is in prison. Mom or Dad, his point of contact on the outside, is now too sick to do that any more. Suddenly, his appeals for assistance come directly to you, the caregiver. "Send me this. Bring me that."

Friends, there are only so many hours in the day. You can only do so much.

I'm not suggesting that you abandon your incarcerated brother or sister. Not at all. But I am asking you to consider your mental and physical health. You don't have to replicate your mother or father's actions with that sibling. As caregiver, you're not obligated to send money to an inmate on behalf of your loved one. You're not obliged to put your 85-year-old mother in a car on a Sunday and drive her three hours to the state penitentiary.

A warning: Be prepared for what happens when you say "no." Your imprisoned relative might get upset with you. He or she might even say, "What do you mean you don't have time for me? What do you mean you won't send any of Mom or Dad's money to me? It's not YOUR money, it's Mom's money! It's Dad's money! You don't care about me! You don't love me! "

Be prepared to be the "bad guy."

That's OK. Each time you deal with the prodigal son or daughter's return, you must ask yourself this question: Is this the old person or the new person?

You must do it to protect your loved one's interests. And to protect yourself.

CHAPTER 9
MEMORIES

Many people experience some changes in their memory as they age. They forget where they parked their car in the grocery store parking lot or struggle to recall the name of someone famous.

That's a common and even expected part of the aging process.

But memory loss and cognitive impairments that disrupt daily life aren't a typical part of aging. They may be signs of dementia-related behavior.

Dementia isn't a specific disease, but rather a range of symptoms associated with memory or thinking problems that are severe enough to affect a person's ability to perform everyday activities. The most common form of dementia is Alzheimer's disease, a progressive and incurable illness that eventually leads to death. In addition to memory issues, signs might include:

Wandering

- The inability to pay bills and manage a household.

- Major personality changes.

- Loss of bowel and bladder control.

- Toward the end, the inability to communicate.

- Other forms of dementia include:

- Vascular dementia, or brain damage caused by impaired blood flow to the brain.

- Lewy body dementia, in which protein deposits form on nerve cells in the brain, impairing movement, thinking and memory.

- Frontal lobe dementia, caused by progressive nerve loss in the brain's frontal region.

If the person for whom you are caring begins to show signs of memory or thinking problems, it's important to discuss the issue with a doctor. The earlier you know the type of dementia, the quicker your medical team can start the proper treatment, which may slow the symptoms.

As a caregiver, you're tasked with deciding when these symptoms progress to the point where your loved one can no longer live alone and is ready for continuous medical care and supervision.

The vast majority of older Americans want to live independently in their own homes. And many seniors who receive assistance at home rely on unpaid family care — a fact of which many of you reading this are already painfully aware. We perform a variety of caregiving activities, including helping with bathing and dressing, meal preparation, medication management, wound care, transportation and more.

What happens when, in addition to all of those things, your loved one can no longer be left alone for any length of time? We're talking about memory loss to a point where it causes serious issues — leaving the stove on, forgetting to turn off the bathtub faucet, letting a pot of water boil over on the stove.

Caregivers, we have to be honest with ourselves: No matter how committed we are to keeping that loved one in his or her own home, there comes a point where it's just too much for one person to handle. We can no longer provide all the care and supervision our loved one needs.

But your loved one says, "No, I want to stay in my own house." I understand that. It's a gut-wrenching decision. Part of you feels guilty about going against your loved one's wishes, and the other part feels relief that someone else will share the weight and responsibility of caring for that person.

That doesn't make you selfish or cold. It makes you human.

When you're dealing with dementia, particularly in the most advanced stage, there's little else you can do but turn outside the family for help. Unless you have unlimited resources and can hire a team of people to watch your loved one 24/7 — and who among us has that kind of money? – you're going to have to place that person in a facility.

My advice: When you do make that decision, be kind to yourself. Don't beat yourself up. And don't let the anger and sadness of your loved one weaken your resolve.

After all, you're doing it for their safety — and your mental health.

***

Make no mistake. Dementia is insidious, robbing our loved ones of their memories.

But it also robs you, the caregiver, of your relationship with that person — something that's especially difficult when your parent is the one experiencing memory issues. In many ways, your mom and dad are the custodians of memories of your earliest childhood experiences. You want to be able to look at your parents and say, "Do you remember the time that I ...?"

It's so incredibly painful when they stare back at you with a blank look on their face.

It's also difficult when your parent, the person who taught you to brush your teeth and tie your shoes, needs your help performing those tasks. You're already stretched by serving as the primary caregiver, but then you have the added psychological burden of reversing roles with your parent. And all the while you're thinking, "Why can't it be like it used to be? When I was the child and she was the adult, and I just played all day? Hopscotch. Baseball. Double Dutch. Basketball.

"Why can't it be that day again, when I was the child, and Mom and Dad took care of *me*?"

This is a very normal reaction to a completely intolerable situation. As you mourn the loss of your loved one to dementia — yes, you'll mourn it like you would a death — you'll likely go through the stages of grief: denial, anger, bargaining, depression and acceptance.

Your relationship with your loved one will be forever changed. Though dementia may have robbed the person you're caring for of his or her memories — and robbed you of your relationship with your loved one — it cannot rob you of your memories.

So remember. Reflect. Think about the time everyone was sitting at the dinner table, laughing. Recall that one special family reunion when your father and your uncles told funny stories until 1 a.m. Spend as much time as you can going back in time to the happiest, most precious memories you have of your loved one.

Most importantly, know that the decisions you're making are in the best interest of your loved one.

And you.

CHAPTER 10
WHEN CAREGIVING ENDS

A while ago, I was talking to a man who had been his wife's primary caregiver for the last five years. He did it all — driving her to appointments, picking up her prescriptions, changing her sheets, bathing her, feeding her.

His wife had just recently died.

As we discussed her passing, I mentioned King Solomon's words about "the appointed time" and my theory that, at some point in our lives, we are either going to take care of someone or someone is going to take care of us.

He agreed.

I talked to him about the period of time — something all of us who provide care think about: "How long, God? How long will I be a caregiver?" We discussed how normal and natural it is for caregivers to feel that the care they're providing is a burden, no matter how much they love the person for whom they are caring.

Then I asked him the question I ask most caregivers: "Were you guilty or relieved when your time as a caregiver ended?"

"Both," he said with such honesty and earnestness that tears welled up in my eyes. "I felt guilty about some of the things I could have done for her but never had time to do. But I also was relieved, Odell. Now I get to live my own life again."

It was the first time someone answered my question that way.

At some point, caregivers, our appointed time will end. Our loved one either will get better and no longer need our care ... or die. Sadly, it usually is the latter.

And that brings us to a subject many of us avoid thinking about, much less discussing: When our appointed time as caregiver is over, how will we deal with the guilt over feeling relieved?

Don't get me wrong. You'll be devastated. But you'll also be thankful that your appointed time as a caregiver has ended. It is possible to experience both emotions — grief and relief — at the same time. A wife, for instance, may sit on the front row of the pew during the funeral, crying real tears, feeling genuine emotions, but thinking, "I miss him, but I thank God for my freedom. I miss him, but I'm so glad to have my life back."

We shouldn't punish ourselves when that happens. Once again, let me give you permission to feel relief with no guilt. You will have traveled a long, hard road by the time your loved one leaves you. There will have been many missed dinners with your partner and children, many hours spent pacing hospital rooms, many sleepless nights filled with work and worry.

With that being said, it's incumbent on us to do our very best so that when our time as a caregiver is over, we won't feel guilty about feeling relieved. We want our conscience to be at peace, not railing against us. We want Mom or Dad to say, "I'm proud of you. I appreciate what you do for me. I know the sacrifices."

How do we do that? It's my hope that "It's My Turn Now" has provided a roadmap for providing loving, compassionate care for your loved one, your family — and yourself:

- Understand that this "appointed time" in your life won't last forever. I know it's hard right now, but it's also temporary. It's an assignment.

- Be honest with your loved one about his or her situation. Discuss what the future holds — both in terms of your ability to provide care and the reality of fulfilling their care directives. To the best of your ability, have this honest conversation without making your loved one feel as though they're a burden. Nothing hurts like hearing your loved one say, "I've lived too long."

- Work hard to build strong relationships with family members. Hold meetings to keep your relatives informed about your loved one's condition, upcoming decisions and financial matters. Put aside any hard feelings you have with your siblings, if only to make things easier for your mother or father while they're sick.

- Don't be afraid — or ashamed — to ask for help. You don't have to do it all, and your loved one deserves care from as many people as possible.

- Make the tough decisions, even if they're unpopular. Yes, it's especially hard when you're making decisions that go against your loved one's wishes. Unfortunately, such matters are up to you as primary caregiver. Just remember, you're doing it with his or her best interests in mind.

- Don't spend energy trying to change things you can't control. This includes your loved one's condition and the behavior of those around you. You're already stretched to the limit. Focus instead on the things you can change.

- Friends, you don't have to be a perfect caregiver. Mommy, Glen and Noddy would tell you that I've been far from perfect in the Cleveland family's journey. But I've tried to follow my own advice, which I hope will lead me to a guilt-free life once my appointed time as a caregiver is over.

That was the case with a friend of mine, who during his mother's long illness was a devoted caregiver, a supportive brother and a thoughtful decision-maker. And when she passed, he knew he had done all he could do.

"Odell," he told me, "I stood at the side of Big Momma's grave, and I felt good because I had no regrets. I did all the things I was supposed to do."

***

I'd like to say just a few words about dealing with your loved one's estate. Now, I'm not a probate attorney, an accountant or an asset manager. I'm a preacher of the Gospels, so it shouldn't surprise you that the guidance I'm offering is more about your soul than your legal responsibilities.

When people leave us, they're supposed to leave wills that tell us how they want to distribute their worldly possessions. I repeat: how they want to do it. Not what their children or grandchildren want. Not what you want. What they want.

If your loved one doesn't have a will, you should urge him or her to create one. For most people without vast amounts of wealth, it's an easy, inexpensive process that will save you a lot of hassles — and ensure that his or her wishes are carried out.

If there is a will, then there's a possibility you'll also be tasked with handling his or her final affairs because you're already acting as your loved one's primary caregiver. That might mean doling out money from an insurance policy; selling a home and divvying up the proceeds; or dividing up jewelry, cars and cash. It also may involve giving small items that hold sentimental value — pictures, clothes and knickknacks — to the correct people.

Sometimes, settling an estate can lead to fights among relatives. I've seen that tragedy play out many times in my professional life, as families turn to their pastor to referee their disputes over the estate.

"It's not fair that Dad left you the house. You've already got a house!"

"Mom named you executor of the estate and left you money. That's not fair!"

It's your loved one's prerogative to distribute the assets how he or she sees fit. And it's your responsibility to bring those plans to fruition. Sadly, not everyone is going to see that as fair.

In fact, a few of you will be in for a fight.

People have told me, "Odell, my sister and my brother — they didn't do anything for Mom. But the second she closed her eyes, there they were. It got so nasty. They wanted what they wanted. And they wanted it all."

Caregivers, if this happens to you — and I certainly hope it doesn't — then my advice is to follow your loved one's will. As executor or administrator of the estate, you really have no other choice. You didn't write the will, yet you are tasked with following through with the plans it lays out. The situation is what the situation is.

You want to talk about unfair? Blaming you for carrying out someone's wishes as mandated by law is the very definition of unfair.

Hopefully, your family members will understand that you are simply the person tasked with a tremendous chore: closing down someone's life. Don't spend a lot of time, energy and effort worrying about whether what you're doing is fair.

And remember: If you follow the law and your loved one's wishes, if you conduct yourself in an ethical and humane way, then you will have no need to feel any guilt — only relief when this one last task is complete.

'IT'S MY TURN NOW' AFTERWORD

A few years ago, our wheelchair-bound Mommy upgraded to a motorized model. She was excited about how much more mobility she would have, both at home and at the adult daycare center where she spends her days while my brother Noddy works.

We were excited for her.

One problem: Mommy had a need for speed. Plus she hadn't quite learned to operate her new machine, either. She was terrorizing people at the daycare — flying down the hall, bumping into things, taking corners too tight.

"Listen, Ms. Glenda," daycare staffers told her, "you've got to slow this thing down."

Mommy sure didn't want to lose that sweet ride: "Dell," she told me in a hushed, worried tone, "they said if I don't learn how to drive this thing, they're going to put me back in the manual wheelchair." So she practiced and practiced, forcing herself to slow down.

And the wheelchair technician adjusted the throttle switch, which ensured that the wheelchair crept.

Suffice to say, the complaints ceased.

Even today, that story makes me smile. It demonstrates everything I love about Mommy: her spirit, her enthusiasm, her determination, her refusal to let health challenges stop her from living a full life.

Mommy's health is stable, but she requires increasing assistance with the activities of daily living. She continues to attend adult day care daily, where she enjoys socializing with her peers. Mommy also attends a weekly service at church, where she has served on the steward board for 20 years. When it's her group's time to serve, she proudly sits in her wheelchair at the front of the church, dressed in all white with her group.

Although Mommy lives 300 miles from Greensboro, my local friends and church family say they feel as though they know her. They check in with me after my visits home, asking for updates on her health and sharing stories about caring for their own ailing loved ones.

Richard Lyons is an elderly gentleman who, with wife Corine, sits a few rows behind me at church, and has for the past eight years. Because of the way I was raised, I always go out of my way to speak to senior members every Sunday morning before the service starts. For years, I never really knew the Lyons as anything more than just a very nice interesting couple — the kind I hope my wife Bev and I will become years from now. It doesn't take much intelligence to realize that Richard has lived a very meaningful life. You just have to watch how he carries himself.

One Sunday, during one of our normal greetings, I asked him what he did before he retired. He smiled and said he would give me a book he wrote that would explain.

"Perfect," I said. "However, I'm a writer also and I will pay you for the book."

He paused for a short period of time. As he pondered my request and looked at me, I just smiled.

"OK," he said.

The next week, he brought the book. And I paid him. Then I started reading about this amazing black teacher-coach who started his career in rural eastern North Carolina when schools were segregated. So I started calling him coach and talked about his life's journey with him.

On Dec. 29, 2019, Greensboro writer and editor Teresa Prout wrote an amazing article in the News & Record of Greensboro newspaper: "It's my turn now: Greensboro reverend writes book about family's experience as caregivers for elderly mother."

The next Sunday, Richard walked up to me and looked me in the eyes and congratulated me on the article. He asked if he could write a poem for my mother. Of course, I said. A week later, he presented me with a large manila envelope that contained the poem, while his wife Corine just smiled.

It's called "A Tribute to Ms. Glenda":

> Sometimes, it's hard for the establishment to hear a different voice,
>
> But through your dogged determination, they didn't have a choice.
>
> However, as your siblings become long-livers
>
> They have all come together to become caregivers.

As they are all working together, they still can become stressed,

Yet they realize through God how much they are blessed.

As Pastor Odell stated and realizes for sure,

The rest of us know, through his efforts, that all is clean and pure.

Although he realizes that he could stay in touch by phone or letter,

A trip home to care for Mom is always better.

Through long distance, other caregivers realize they can't always be there,

Their blessings will surely reach you through intercessory prayer.

Also, others can only imagine that your early love was strong and tender,

The indelible love left by Pastor Odell and siblings will always be there, Ms. Glenda.

For to know that you are loved and care for from near and far away,

We are spiritually sure that we all will be reunited on salvation day.

I continue to be amazed by Richard's poem. And I don't just mean because of the exceptional quality. He really understands my family's situation — our challenges and our joys, our struggles and our prayers.

As I write this, Noddy is still living with Mommy, but plans to move in the near future. He's working from home due to the COVID-19 outbreak, which also has forced Mommy to stay at home. And although Glen's health is improving, her challenges continue.

I'm forever indebted to Noddy and Glen for their life-long devotion to Mommy. They're the glue that keeps our family together. Caring is in their DNA. Love is in their DNA. It's inside them.

My siblings and I continue to keep our relationship as joint caregivers strong and healthy by "overcommunicating," a Cleveland family trait, I suppose. There's always something to discuss: Mommy's transportation to adult daycare. The results from doctor visits. The status of her medication. And, of course, money. The list goes on and on.

Whenever possible, the three of us talk about these matters face to face — I drive from Greensboro to Charleston every three or four weeks to see Mommy. But in between, there are countless calls and texts. About minor problems. About major issues. About everything.

We keep each other informed. We have the difficult conversations. We speak the hard truths.

We have planned ahead, too, for the day when Mommy leaves us. She has discussed arrangements with us for her funeral and burial. We've discussed who will serve as administrator of her estate. Mommy made that easier by naming her executor in her will. We've talked about financial matters, including paying her final bills and dividing her belongings.

We pray that that day is far, far away.

For now, I'm focused on providing Mommy with the best possible care, dealing with crises as they arise, being kind to my siblings and to myself. I owe that to Mommy, to Noddy and to Glen.

Because it's my turn now.